I Still Want It

Derrick Jaxn

TABLE OF CONTENTS

PREFACE

I want to fall in love again. This time, without the fear of falling on my face. I want deep conversations without a fear of trusting too much and to hold without a fear of having to let go.

I want someone I don't have to watch my back with, because we have each other. Effortless smiles and laughs until our cheeks are sore. I want to cuddle up on cold nights watching movies until those movies are watching us.

I want to make love, real love. The kind where you'd better stretch, put your hair in a high ponytail, and have water bottles nearby because nobody will be able to walk to the fridge afterwards. I want the climax to only be half time, not the finish line. And I want conversation and complimenting each other on a job well-done, until we're ready for more.

I want her to wake up because I'm too loud in the kitchen trying to surprise her with breakfast in bed. I want to see her put on my shirt because she can't find her clothes, and when she goes to comb her hair, I want to come up and hug her from behind. Whisper something funny in her ear and watch her laugh in the bathroom mirror as we admire how good we look together.

"People my age want to be a cute couple.
I'd rather be a winning team."

I STILL WANT IT

Everybody needs somebody to confide in

Or maybe just...lie back and chill with,

and after a few minutes of silence

Turn and ask what they were thinking about

To see if you were on their mind.

And chances are you would be,

Because that's what best friends are like.

But I wanna be more than friends.

I wanna do all the corny stuff

Like going to the state fair

And going broke on games trying to

win her huge teddy bears.

You know, because girls like that.

And if I'm lucky, it'll be too cold

to not hold hands.

She'll be happy either way because

she's with me. She'll understand.

And I'll listen to her.

I'll write her poems to show her I did.

When I mess up,

I'll swallow my pride, apologize,

And give her a soft forehead kiss.

Or maybe, wait 'til she goes to work,

Fill her car up with her favorite flowers.

You know, a nice gesture

to show her I care about her.

Because I do. I mean…I will.

I'll treat her right. Like a queen.

I won't just treat her like a queen,

I'll get on one knee

And give her the crown too: an engagement ring.

Yeah…I'm into that whole marriage thing.

Not just the wedding,

but the children, the fussing,

The sleeping with no clothes on

In case we're having wet dreams

we wanna turn into a reality

Until we're turning the alarm off…

All of it. I want that.

I don't know if it's outdated

or not "cool" anymore but,

I still want it.

Nobody wants to spend their days trying to stop missing someone. I'm no exception. No superhero, although I pretend to be sometimes. But deep down, I think we all crave someone who lets us take off our super cape and expose our human flaws. Even after we've tried and tried and mistakenly thought we were done for good. That part of us that wants the calm before every other storm in our past to last for the rest of our lives; it lives on.

In my youth, I set out to kill it. Promiscuity, lies, apathy; you name the weapon, I used it mercilessly but to absolutely no avail. Painful lessons learned and some scars that'll never heal molded a new faith in love. A faith manifested by exposure to women who revealed to me the full evolution of human beings in their strongest form. The amazing thing was that they didn't even realize it.

GOD HASN'T FORGOTTEN YOU

Pretty girl, big smile, bright future.

Came across a guy who promised

to do everything but lose you.

Skeptical at first, but still,

you gave him a chance to be different,

but when your period stopped it wasn't long

before he, too, came up missing.

But first, you broke the news,

and he tried to talk you into an abortion.

Telling you how he's not ready to be a father,

and how you had no right to force him.

How you were only trying to trap him

when really you tried to trust him.

He put his name on what was in your pants

but denied the life that was in your stomach.

Fast forward... you're grown now,

but never forgot how that felt,

So you refuse to abandon your

child even if you have no help,

But the world's still blaming you

for that coward's decision.

Calling you a *baby momma*

like having no help were your intentions.

But you don't fit the stereotype

of the ones they show on TV

You're not out spending child support

on expensive weaves.

Matter of fact, you'd rather starve

than see your child not eat.

But society doesn't see that

or the nights you cry yourself to sleep

Not because you "need a man"

or that you're ready to give up,

But because your child deserves two parents

while you're only capable of being one.

Struggling to pay for daycare

but you need it to keep a steady job.

Yet you get called *baby momma drama*

for making a man take care of his own child.

While sometimes you wonder

why nobody knows your pain.

I'm here to tell you, single mothers

and superheroes are one and the same.

Keep your head up, you survived

what few could have gotten through,

And that alone is proof that

God hasn't forgotten you.

Loyalty. I think it's one of the most beautiful concepts in the world, but in the wrong hands it can be the most destructive effort there is. Especially for women who love hard, because the bigger your heart is, the more of it there is to break. And then you have people who come along with intentions of breaking every piece there is along with your trust and sanity. Somehow those assholes come find women who try to love them through their imperfections, and they ruin them forever. They don't just come with baggage, they come with a wrecking ball, but the woman they've chosen remains loyal, revealing reality a few minutes too late.

*"Too many good girls going hard for guys
who deserve to be left."*

THE RIDER

She was a rider,

never complained while he drove

Just kept silent,

even helped him keep his eyes on the road,

but then the mileage

became too much for her to keep going.

He kept switching lanes without knowing

and was losing control.

So then she cried out,

"If we need to pull over,

just let me know.

Forget a ticket, you keep this up

and we ain't gon' make it home."

He turned the radio louder,

drowned out the tears of her soul,

So she reached for her seatbelt

just as they hit the consequences

of his lifestyle head-on.

She was a rider.

"The worst thing you can ever do is walk into somebody's heart, make yourself at home, and rob them of their trust the moment they let their guard down."

TECHNICALLY SPEAKING

She always seemed to get looked over,

Hung out with a few dudes

but not one would hold her.

She was one of the homies

who never was brought home,

And if it wasn't for her cousin's kindness,

she would've went to prom alone.

Got to college, put on makeup

for the very first time.

Skinny jeans, low-cut shirt,
now she think she fine.
Athletes and Greeks
must've thought the same thing.
Problem is they wanted to undress
everything but her mind.

She wasn't with it.

So she went home over
Christmas break, saw an old friend.
He noticed the changed in her,
decided to get close again.
She knew she could trust 'im.
She'd known him for years
But also noticed that all of a sudden
he was acting weird.

She asked him why and he laughed it off,

told her she was tripping.

Told her to stop acting brand new,

then they would go back to chilling.

Things went back to cool

for the next couple of days

But the break was about over

so he asked for just one more date.

Picked her up, took her for

about an hour drive

She didn't ask where,

always had been down to ride.

Her phone died and she still didn't know

where they were headed.

Got curious what the reason was

that he still didn't tell her.

So she broke the silence and asked,

because things were looking scary

He said, "It's a surprise but don't worry.

We'll be there in a second."

Pulled over to the side of the road

and turned the engine off.

Told her if she wanted a ride home,

then she'd have to let him pop her cherry…

She needed to get home.

The next semester would start the next day.

But she never planned on losing

her virginity that way.

Still she complied to try

and get all over with

Hoping that later on she could sleep it off,

move on and forget.

But it didn't work that way,

so she went and saw the school counselor

Who helped her press rape charges

except she'd already taken a shower
Scrubbing for hours trying to rid herself
of the guilt and shame
Even though she wasn't the least to blame.

Filed a report anyway,
told the story to policemen.
First thing they asked is
"Why didn't you just leave then?"
And, "How sure are you that your period
isn't why you were bleeding?"
Then, "How come nobody around
was able to hear you screaming?"
They said, "Rape victims come with bruises,
and we don't see them.
So maybe you're just feeling a little guilty
from a regretful agreement
Because if you didn't say no, then it wasn't rape...
technically speaking."

"Don't let them teach you how to love them until you've already practiced on yourself."

BEAUTY'S NOT MEASURED ON A SCALE

She exists inside of the hearts of many.
The girl who was told

it ain't right if it ain't skinny.
The girl who was convinced

only one type was pretty
And it hurt at first, but now she's grown,

she can't feel it.

See, she's a star to the man

who would give her the moon
But until she loves herself,

that won't do her any good

Because when he tells her she's beautiful,

she thinks he's a fool,
And all she sees in the mirror

is how much weight she should lose.

Fad diets, P90x,

Slim Fast, the color black
Photoshop, holding her breath,

looser clothing, body wraps.
She's seen it all, done it all,

and every one of them seemed to fail
Because the girl never learned

beauty's not measured on a scale.

No butterfly has ever flown without paying its dues in the dirt. I'd like to think I'm somewhere in that stage where my cocoon is loosening and facing the fear of new heights, motivated by memories of my dirt days. I'm not ashamed by them. Amused at times? Yes. But ashamed, no. In fact, I'm proud of that modern-day-me prototype because even in its most crude and premature form, it had the potential to grow into who I am now and who I'm on my way to being.

"I can admit, I have pride issues. I hate asking people for help and I hate admitting when I'm not okay."

SOMEBODY I'M NOT

My professor concluded,

"So students, never try to be

somebody you're not."

So, I raised my hand and asked,

"What if you have a reason to

that you can't live without?"

The class turned and laughed

but I kept a straight face.

I said, "What if changing

is the only way she'll stay?

And you can't let her go because

while you can always find another pretty face,

the memories simply can't be replaced."

My professor asked,

"Are you suggesting that one should pretend?"

I answered, "No, sir. I'm suggesting that I'll do anything

if it means keeping my best friend."

The room fell silent,

with all eyes on me.

I said, "Professor, I'm sure you'll agree

that God sometimes blesses us with things

or people we don't deserve.

Well, mine was her.

Not knowing what you got till it's gone

is a lesson I don't want to learn.

But currently,

I can't afford my woman's worth.

But if losing who I am now

so I can build a future with her is necessary

then I'll give anything and everything

to become a man who's ready.

Please, help me. I'm running out of time.

What sociologists have you studied

who can turn me into somebody I'm not?

A man with no scars from the past,

no strings attached,

no trust issues, or lust issues

when skin-tight jeans walk past.

The polygamous habits I developed

to be accepted as a "player"

are the very things I'm afraid

will eventually cause me to play her.

You see, I don't make it easy to love me,

but she does it anyway.

She stayed down from the beginning

when I didn't have a dime to my name.

While my fake friends turned their backs

on me and walked away,

she grabbed my hand

told me to kneel down and pray.

That everything would be all right,

if I just kept the faith.

And it worked.

Now I'm better because of her,

but still not who she needs me to be.

Somebody who knows how to communicate

and swallow his pride,

who knows she's lying when she says she's fine

because he can see it in her eyes.

Somebody who never forgets to compliment

when she switches her hairstyle.

Tell me, professor.

How can I become that guy?

Don't get me wrong, I treat her right,

I'm just not right for her.

But I'll guard her heart even if it means

giving my life for her.

I just need a sign that it's hope

for a troubled man to change

because life without my baby

just wouldn't be the same.

She's all I got.

So please tell me you can help me

become somebody I'm not."

"The sooner you realize that giving everything you have still won't be enough for some, the sooner you stop giving it to the wrong ones."

CONFESSIONS OF AN AIN'T-SHIT NIGGA

Me:

Society always tryna

help you recognize me

Telling lies on me, but honestly

I'm tired of having to disguise me.

Hmph. I'm an ain't-shit nigga.

But real enough to admit it.

I got feelings nobody ever considers.

Hell yeah, I want sex,

but it wasn't my decision.

Physical arousal happens

without my permission.

So don't blame me

for the flesh I was given.

I'm obedient to nature,

not politically correct decisions.

Now, when we first met,

everything was all cool,

So why do I get the feeling

that I'm auditioning for you?

How come I got everything to lose

and everything to prove

With no guarantee I'll even be

the one you will choose?

Her:

Be a man, the responsibility is yours

If you want me, then show me.

Open all of my doors.

Pay the tab and the tip for the dates

I LET you take me on.

You can't expect an allowance

without first doing your chores.

Me: Wait, if sex is a reward

then why am I the lone recipient?

If your love is an allowance,

then what makes mine some kind of punishment?

A red flag that I'm in it

for all the wrong reasons?

You're sending mixed signals,

but I'm wrong because I receive them?

I admire your beauty

and I would never disrespect it

But how am I the enemy

for acting on my affection?

Now, if you don't want the attention

then cool, I'll respect it.

But those half-naked mirror pics

gave me the wrong impression.

I don't judge books by their cover,

but I always read the title.

Yours is saying triple X,

but you call it the Holy Bible.

You expose what you want ignored,

And I "ain't shit" for wanting more

Like, you're telling me to keep knocking

while holding open the door.

You show me how sexy you are,

and I can't show you the same thing?

No, this ain't a guilt trip,

you don't owe me a damn thing.

Her:

I'm not perfect but why can't

you just accept me?

Me:

Because I'm allergic to bullshit,

and when you talk, I sneeze.

Her:

You ain't shit and

I deserve the best.

My momma told me

to never settle for less.

Any man with good sense

would recognize that I'm blessed,

So you can take your little speech

and exit to the left.

Me:

Sure, but when the next one comes along,

he'll be nothing like me.

He'll know what you like.

He'll do and say as you please.

He'll learn from my mistake

of giving you honesty.

He'll fall right in your trap,

then take off with your cheese.

See, you want a queen's riches
while competing with bad bitches
To appeal to a "real nigga",
asking why real men are missing.
You blush when I like your pics
and compliment your every curve
But get mad when my actions start
speaking louder than my words...
Or rather not mad, but proud, in fact,
to reject them.
Because society will agree,
I'm just a "slave to my erection
whose character is flawed
and in need of correction."
Then pat you on the back
and applaud your deception.
See, it's chicks like you
who give hoes a bad rep.
At least they have the decency

to exude and then give sex.

But you're false advertising

so an "ain't-shit nigga" buys it

Then complain about him

not giving you respect.

Her:

You come at me like

I'm doing you wrong.

I'm just tryna get to know you,

am I taking too long?

You just like these other men,

I give it up then you're gone

Get what you want and disappear

like magic tricks from a wand.

Me:

It's about more than that.

It's about reciprocation.

But you sayin' I ain't shit

for wanting mutual admiration.

I'm wondering the real reason
why you're testing my patience.
So you can brag about rejecting me
for Twitter ovations?
Physical or emotional,
it's all a part of you,
But you're showing me one half
telling me to love all of you.
I always say how I feel
and you say you need proof
But when my actions speak up
it makes you uncomfortable.
Now, I don't have a problem
if we wait for sex,
But is it me, or everyone else
that you're trying to impress?
That value of a good woman
can exceed any wealth
but don't demand more respect

than what you're giving yourself.

You get drunk every weekend

always losing your phone.

It's been years since you've

worn your hair naturally grown.

Rappers call you a bitch and you say

"Ooh, that's my song"

But if you get treated as such,

then you act like you've been wronged.

You think your actions are harmless,

but they call the wrong attention.

Your personality is cool,

but consistency is missing.

Instead of rising to your worth,

you're playing down to the competition.

But who am I to say?

I'm just an "ain't-shit nigga".

"When walking away from someone means walking towards your true potential, take that step every single time."

WORK IT OUT

How we gon' work it out if you ain't never tryna hear it,

or "got time for my shit". Just take a second to listen

The back-and-forth that leads to silent treatments and

You grabbing your keys, telling me that you leaving is

Getting old. But I'm not ready to throw the towel in.

I'd rather wipe the sweat from our brow and try again.

I'm down for joint prayer or therapy with a specialist

Or foreplay for however long and sexual healing

Because it's hard now, but baby, there'll be better days.

What good is sunshine if we never feel the rain?

If you walk out that door, I'll probably kick it down,

Not because I'm crazy, I just realize who I'm crazy about

I don't need a second chance, I wasn't finished with the first one.

We ain't perfect, but I think that we should work it out.

"Some of us wake up every morning thinking about someone who doesn't lose an ounce a sleep for the pain they put us through."

TWO CAN PLAY THAT GAME

Her:

You don't deserve to be hurt,

you done did wrong before

Meeting up with ya ex on Christmas break

when you went home.

Probably fucked her, didn't you?

Never mind, don't answer.

You just gon' lie again

and that's just gon' make me madder.

See, that's yo problem,

you lie like it's ya second language

Then come thinking you can piss on my leg

and tell me it's raining.

I ain't stupid,

Well, maybe a little for trusting you

but you sadly mistaken thinking

I'm home waiting for you.

See while you was out,

running the streets and acting single,

I called up this cutie that

gave me his number a few days ago

He looked at me like you used to do

back in the day

But that was then. As of now

just know that two can play that game.

Anyway, we talked on the phone

for a couple of minutes.

He said you must be insane

to be out chasing other women

He said you losing with those other chicks,

with me you could be winning.

Then he asked if he could show me

how you was no competition

So I said yeah, hung up,

texted him the address.

I knew when you'd be home

and we had plenty time left.

One thing led to another,

And, um, well, you know the rest.

An hour later you pulled up,

thinking I was asleep in the bed

So now you know.

Pick yo' mouth up off the flo'.

You had yo chance once befo'.

Now it's time for you to go.

And those were the last words

I ever heard her say

Word is she's still tryna find love

but trust issues get in the way

When a good guy does come,

she never can tie up her lace.

I mean she can't stop tripping off the fear

of falling back on her face.

Believe it or not,

she was once my little angel.

We thought we were gonna make it,

contemplated names for future babies,

Moved in together. I even used to help her

set the dinner table.

I could smell the food cooking from the room

so good that I could taste it

But as time went on, I got complacent,

Forgot the basics,

Leaving late at night

and wouldn't say shit.

Made plans just to break them

Lost count of the second chances

she gave me.

Eventually got caught cheating

and things ain't ever been the same since.

So everything that happened to her heart,

was my fault. I gotta live with that guilt

Yeah, two can play that game,

but nobody ever wins.

As cliché as it sounds,

I wish I could do it all over again

Because no girl deserves that pain

it takes to turn her into a bitch.

"When you truly love someone, you want the best for their future.
Even if it won't include you."

FRIEND ZONE

Had a talk with the old me.

Mentally he doesn't announce when he's coming.

He just makes himself at home and won't leave.

But it's cool because he knows me,

Knows I got potential.

Knows I had nothing but the best intentions

since the day that I met you.

Since then I've gone from him

to a pretty good man,

but I guess my good gotta be better

before I'm more than just a friend.

I been in this zone for far too long,

with feelings that won't let go,

butterflies that just won't go home

like...Roger's ass.

They heard you knocking on my heart

when we were balling at the park

on some *Love and Basketball* shit,

You stay calling me your bro,

even though I was so close

helping you with your free throws,

but hey, I loved it.

I was the one that you confided in

when your man was less than a man to you.

I was stuck between comforting you with dishonesty

or having you hating me

if I just told you the truth.

The truth, that you needed to

leave his sorry ass,

That even a blind man could

see that you were all that.

And the truth that if your heart was broken,

then you could use mine

Because you already had it

and I didn't want it back.

But then I'd come off as an opportunist

waiting for something good in your life

that I could ruin.

I guess that makes me fake.

Maybe I should've kept it real

but I just couldn't do it

So we sat and talked.

I held you for like an hour.

And you moved on, continued looking in others

for a chemistry like ours.

I watched you grow into a beautiful woman,

Took pride in every accomplishment,

Fell in love from a distance but

respectfully remained quiet.

I reminisce with the old me

about you all the time

He won't let me live my days of doing those

"she loves me, she loves me nots"

The ones I used to tell you

was for the girl up the block.

Damn, now that I think about it,

I lied to you a lot.

I guess some things never change,

like this friend zone I managed to get in

Now, I'm fake smiling at the front row of your wedding.

Trying to be grateful to at least be your best friend.

While deciding if it's in either of our best interests

for me to ever see you again.

"Love someone because you're ready, not lonely."

I CAN'T MAKE YOU LOVE ME

I can't make you love me,

but if I could I would.

It's too late for you to leave him but,

maybe you should.

I know that's weak of me to say,

but I don't always claim to be strong.

You told me when it's real, it's right,

so what I'm saying ain't wrong.

I pray for you every night

before I pray for me.

Think about you right after that

till I fall asleep

just in case it's my last chance,

'cuz I don't always dream,

but in the days I did

you always believed.

Could see in me

what the world looked over.

Pointing at the TV saying

that's gonna be me as we would chill up on the sofa,

We would laugh it off, and I'd continue to hold you,

thinking how one day I'd prove you right

and let the whole word know it…

But that's all gone now.

Maybe it's better if I put this phone down,

'Cuz if you picked up while he was still around,

I can't say for sure that you would hear me out.

So just hear me out.

I STILL WANT IT

You know I ain't the one

for all of the reminiscing,

but I ain't no liar, and I'd be lying

if I said I wasn't missing

those late-night visits

when we would not have sex

'cuz we lost track of time just chilling.

With Lauryn Hill on repeat,

as she sang

how I was in it for just "that thing"

but you knew better

'cuz I showed you every chance you granted.

Ya mom didn't like me

but ya pops thought I was well-mannered.

Every chance you got you made plans of meeting me

and I made sure my taper was right,

my shirt wrinkle-free, got cologne from my step-pops

so that you'd remember me,

and if time is money

I took you on spending sprees.

Hated to leave

but we had to,

missing you

before I had you.

Never could stay mad at you,

ya sense of humor made me laugh at you

till we switched the subject,

but I was off budget.

Knew your worth back then

but couldn't afford to love you.

So I fell back, then we fell off.

Too little too late

I was already in the middle of a free fall

deep in love with the thought

of being Mr. Right.

Now, I'm rough landing on reality

seemingly every single night

with this bottle in my hand.

Android in the other.

Thinking if I'd rather respect you got a man,

or not regret dialing your number.

Because you're all gone now.

Maybe it's better if I put this phone down

'Cuz even if you picked up while he's not around,

the rules changed and I ain't allowed to need you right now.

"Giving someone your heart isn't supposed to leave you heartless."

LETTER TO MY EX

Fuck him. And you.

I hope his dick is small and

he comes too soon.

I hope his snoring keeps you up at night

and it makes you late for school.

On the low, I hope he's peeping ya homegirl

and thinks she's cute.

I hope the feeling is mutual

till the point y'all can't be cool

But I hope you find out

by catching him staring

in front of everybody,

your pastor and your parents.

I hope you get so embarrassed.

Matter of fact, I hope you catch him cheating

and he says, "sharing is caring".

I hope you dump his sorry ass

just to find out you're pregnant

And I hope it's a baby boy and he

and his dad look exactly the same.

I hope after meeting his dad's girlfriend

he calls you by her name.

Some say Karma's a bitch,

others say she's a little insane.

I say if I see her, I'm sliding her some money

and sending her your way.

Sincerely Yours.

*"Getting hurt isn't the only way to get trust issues.
Playing someone and believing they're
probably playing you will do it too."*

I HAD A DREAM

I had a dream last night

that I crashed your wedding.

Everybody turned and looked at me

the moment that I stepped in.

Each bridesmaid had pulled out a butter knife,

And the groomsmen took off their jackets

so they could fight.

Then the police came

and took me to jail, but

I broke out and made it just in time

for the reception.

Saw you and your husband

getting ready to cut the cake.

Then I grabbed a handful

and mushed it in his face.

Right then you had to step between

me and ya whole family

'Cuz you already knew what would happen

if they were to get their hands on me.

And ya husband couldn't believe his eyes

That the man who ruined his wedding day

was being protected by his bride.

It all happened so fast

that even you couldn't explain why.

But there was no doubt when he looked up

and saw my smile

Extra wide, I even sucked some icing

off the tip of my thumb

To send the message that

he wasn't the only one.

Plus I was wearing his shirt I got out y'all

closet the other night.

It was too small at first,

but I stretched it out just right.

If you're wondering why I'd do that,

the answer is I never planned to,

But things happen when being the side-guy

doesn't come with a manual.

"When someone doesn't leave your mind,
it's usually because they're somewhere hiding in your heart."

CONGRATULATIONS

I'm so happy for you,

glad to see it happen for you

He gives you the smile you had

back when we would laugh in school.

When we were optimistic about our future

before the distance had come between

And watered down our communication

to kisses through computer screens.

But I am happy for you.

It'd be selfish of me to think otherwise

Or human rather, because humans

have these things called minds

And minds have one-way entry

for women your type.

Those one-of-a-kind,

would-love-it-if-it-she-could-be-my-wife

I mean...scratch that. I promised myself

I wouldn't become *that* guy,

The guy who struggles to give up

when he knows he deserved a try

Because that's not what friends are for,

even if they were there before

He came along. You're so flawlessly flawed,

I guess no man could ignore.

Still, I can't forget those morning calls

to hear your voice

as I laughed at the raspiness.

And when I asked if you wanted breakfast

you'd perk right up and gladly say, yes.

Then you'd show up late seven minutes exactly

in your pea coat and pajama pants

With your scarf around your neck,

eyes glowing like the sunset

See I told you I'd remember,

I also told you my heart was yours

I even scroll through old text messages

still saved in my old phone

When I was telling you to hold on

and the day would come again when we'd be close

But until that time just put on my old jersey

so that you don't feel alone.

We even kissed in the rain

like they sing about in love songs

And sat talking in the driveway

about nothing all night long.

Feelings fade, memories don't,

and that'll be my only regret

But if tomorrow never comes

and this is my last breath,

I must say, I'm happy for you.

Just as happy as a good friend should be.

I didn't mean to hold up your marriage.

Pastor, *now* I will forever hold my peace.

At some point I had to grow up. So did my priorities, my values, my ambitions, and my taste. If I was going to be anything for my future children to want to emulate or leave a legacy my loved ones would be proud of, I would have to change. I couldn't be spiteful and petty forever… well, I could. But it wasn't going to do anything to break the cycle, a cycle many of us get in when we feel like we're not wrong for being hurt. But we miss the part where holding on to that pain only hurts those who try to love us from that point on. And with that, a thought crossed my mind…

"Everyone who wonders why they even try secretly hopes someone comes along whose actions say, ' This is why.'"

POINTLESS

Do the heartless deserve love?

Do the numb deserve to feel again?

Do the lonely deserve hugs?

Do their scars deserve to heal again?

It's an unfair decision when you didn't pick the choices,

But nobody deserves to feel that wanting something real

is pointless.

In that time, I noticed that racial tensions in the country became more evident by the day. Social media only added fire to the flame that was bigotry, giving every ignorant fool with a voice a chance to spew their hatred and leaving those who weren't racist to feel obligated to separate themselves from that pack. Fortunately, life dealt me a colorful hand of best friends from several different cultures. We celebrated our differences because it gave us a first-hand look into each other's cultural norms, but there was one particular instance that left a bad taste in my mouth with one of them. My now former friend told me that he was willing to excuse the color of my skin, and the tone he said it with was a mistakenly charitable one. I didn't see why someone needed to see through something that I was born with in order to appreciate me, and I didn't hesitate to make that clear.

"We don't have to be one race in order to exercise one love for every race."

CROWN

Him:

There's only one race in this world,

and that's human.

If you get treated differently,

maybe it's because of things that you're doing.

Here you go playing the race card

just because you're black.

Well, I, for one, don't see color

and you should be happy about that.

Me:

Let me be clear, I'm just as brown as the oak tree

they hung my great-grandfather from

When white people said, "boo"

and he had too much courage to run.

Strong like the noose,

that held the weight of his body

Before they soaked his toes in kerosene

and set him on fire.

My melanin is deep like bites

from the German shepherds

That Grandmama stitched up

so it wouldn't get infected

Because my Granddad couldn't be phased

by those water cannons

Out there freedom fighting for his rights

when he got tired of politely asking.

I'm just as dark as the bruises

on the bottom of my daddy's feet

Working holes into his shoes

so the family could eat.

Worked just as hard as his white counterparts

but got paid less

Just to be told, "Don't like it?

Find a job somewhere else."

See, within my color is my history,

history houses my roots,

So if you won't acknowledge my color,

then you can't acknowledge my truth.

You wouldn't walk up to a king

and say that you don't see his crown,

So don't walk up to me

and say that you don't see my brown.

That exchange further set the tone for how I would have to navigate the world. I think some people have the right idea, the whole colorblind concept that is. But we're just a few hundred years of slavery, Jim Crow, and mass incarceration too late for that. And honestly, that colorless world is boring. I want to appreciate the people around me because of their differences, not in spite of them. But what if nobody got to hear the side of my differences that made me beautiful, only the side that made me okay to hate? Better yet, what about the women in my life who looked like me? The ones who raised me, took care of me when I was sick, taught me right from wrong, fought for me when I got bullied, supported me when I had nothing, and cheered for me on every accomplishment? What if nobody told their side of the story? What about my nieces and future daughters? Would they have the confidence to grow up in this world knowing they deserved the best if everyone looked at them and only saw the stereotype? Even if they did have the confidence, would they be left to settle for less because the world didn't know any better? These questions haunted me for weeks as I realized how sick this world was with ignorance. Only truth could be the medicine, and from experience, I had some to share when it came to black women.

"No matter how much love I get from newcomers,
I'll never forget
those who were there from the beginning. And if my
newcomers are here
to stay, they'll respect that."

BLACK GIRL FLY

She gets told that her hair is unprofessional

and her body's too sexual,

That if she'd just straighten it and cover up

she wouldn't be so unacceptable.

People are surprised at her poise

and the fact that she's intellectual

Because she doesn't smack her gum

and roll her neck like she's expected to

And the ideal beauty pedestal

don't belong to girls who look like her

Even when it comes to her own brothers,

and deep down that hurts

Like, she's a default choice

by men she grew up being taught to put first.

Then her sisters feel privileged to be light-skinned,

as if dark skin is a curse.

Businesses won't promote her up the ladder

but promote products to her to buy,

And she's always welcome on reality TV

because people love a good black cat fight.

Respectfully she'll decline

just to scroll down her timeline

And get mocked left and right

with people saying how, "Bitches be like"

She's told she can give birth to a black man,

but not desired by one.

She can get sexed by a white man,

and should spend her life tryna get wifed by one,

But being sought out and respected,

courted with a genuine connection

that's manifested and invested in

by a man is asking too much.

When she doesn't look for a handout,

they tell her that she's being ungrateful.

When she rejects sympathy,

she's seen as bitter and hateful

At times she questions if it's really worth it

to be so strong.

The more she stands tall

the more she's a target to try and make fall

But then she remembers,

through the voice of her God-given intuition

That if it wasn't for her,

then there would be no human existence

And while her aesthetic blessings

are far from her definition, women

all over pay doctors to make their bodies

do their best black girl rendition.

As Queen Hatshepsut

she was a successful ruler in Egypt

And even as a slave woman

she led thousands to freedom.

She revolutionized civil rights

all while being seated,

And presently, her mentee

is the most powerful man of the free world.

The lies that blind society

were also meant to fog her mirror

To only show her a pretty picture

and not the true depth of her potential

So that she could accept what is given

and pass that down to her children,

But through trying to break her

they only caused her spirit to strengthen

So her vision is clearer.

Now she's one of the most college-educated

And employed at higher rates than

even her own brothers who hated,

And for those of us smart enough to see

that with her we're a stronger team

She's the glue of black families

who're bringing back our queens and our kings.

She's Black Girl Fly.

Along with lies that needed to be dispelled about black women, came glorification of the worst qualities in my own brothers that needed to be put in proper perspective. It's crazy to think that at one time, a few of these things used to be what I considered "cool", but at some point in my cocoon of adolescence, I came to my senses. Unfortunately, not everybody else did. I never considered myself an activist until I looked up the definition. An **activist** is a person who campaigns for some kind of social change. I was indeed that. Not only for my culture, not just for love and relationships, but also our understanding on what made a man "real".

*"When you have love for what's real,
you must separate it from its impersonators."*

REAL NIGGAS VS. REAL MEN

Real niggas talk down on the same "Thots"
that they chase.

Real men would rather keep a smile on a loyal
woman's face.

Real niggas want a girl who only rolls weed and
shakes her ass.

Real men need a woman who's conscious and has class.

Real niggas get a check and can't wait to cop a new chain.

Real men close deals and put properties in their name.

Real niggas stay flashing stacks on the gram.

Real men got investments and 401k plans.

Real niggas proudly rep the streets with red and blue
flags

But get in public and be ashamed to hold their girl's
hand.

Real men might be from the streets but they find their
way out.

So they can move they moms too, and surprise her with a
new house.

Real niggas think Netflix at the crib & DiGiorno is a date

Hoping she'll get too sleepy and agree to stay.

Real men make plans, tell her to be ready by eight,

Take her out, and though she got her own, refuses to let
her pay.

Real niggas gotta mixtape but can't read a contract

Swear they nice with words,

but use there, their, and they're in the wrong context.

Real men are intelligent with or without a degree

And instead of tryna buy your affection,

they'll stimulate you mentally.

Real niggas hit the club but

won't attend their child's PTA meetings.

Real men raise their kids and don't go a day without seeing 'em.

Real niggas love to stunt with their J's and their iPhones.

Real men know being real isn't an app you can download.

"Being a player is all about getting women to believe in you just for them to realize you were fake from the beginning. Who made that cool?"

PROUD LAME

Not too interested in TV

and the Internet is full of spilled tea.

Meanwhile I'm so lame I still enjoy dates at the café

asking for extra crème

To make my coffee mocha brown.

Like the queen smiling back at me

Talking about our crowns and how we wanna add jewels

to them by achieving our dreams.

DERRICK JAXN

I know that makes me lame,

in a world where the cool kids don't have goals

Ready to retire after a few tattoos,

some new shoes, and an iPhone

Where the sidechick claims to be feminist

because she's supposedly in control

And where dudes will die for their hood

but will leave a woman to raise their son on her own.

As I began growing mentally, I read about men who did the same and wondered how they dealt with the reality that the world wasn't holding its breath and waiting on them to get their shit together. That part of the process of transitioning into manhood scared me the most. Like, would what I was preparing myself for this entire time be there when I finally made it on the other side?

"The truth hurts. But lies leave scars."

JUST GIVE ME A CHANCE TO GET TO YOU

I know you get tired of being alone

Scrolling through your phone

Hoping a text will come through

From a guy who was just "thinkin' 'bout you".

Tired of getting looked past

As if your qualities are made of glass

That guys look through on to the next chick's ass,

Because while they're doing it for the gram,

Your momma raised you with class,

But your A Plus in that

Can't cuddle so now you're thinking, why pass?

Well, I'll tell you.

You're only collecting emotional scars

By freely giving your body when waiting's too hard.

And even the realest man can't fit his heart

Through the bars of your guard,

So it does more than just protect you

From those looking to sex you

It also keeps what could be special

From ever having a chance to.

So while it feels like your time is being wasted

By not sexually leveraging your body

even though you could

Just know that a man who loves you

will still pull away from the table

If he looks at you and sees

your plate is already full.

"To know her is not just to love her. To know her is to also wonder how in the hell she's still standing."

YOU AMAZE ME

It's a wonder how you're still breathing

Through all those tears it took

for you to leave him,

But your hope in something real

drowned despite you being alive.

Yeah, you believe in God,

You prayed and kept faith,

but never got thrown a lifeline.

See, I've been there...When you can't trust

it's easy not to give a fuck

Or at least pretend you don't

to keep your hopes from getting up

But I'm not gullible enough to think

you'd actually rather be this way.

Heartless because men seem

to only know the right things to say

With actions that never follow,

their hearts turn out to be hollow

You know all men ain't the same,

but how to hurt you seems to be something they all know.

Nobody ever said it would be easy,

but you wonder if it's worth it

Constantly pressured to perfect the ways

to give love even although no one returns it.

And while a part of me wishes I

could make everything different

It's best to create your happy now

so you won't spend your life waiting for your happy ending.

"Don't be afraid to cry. Tears water the soil your soul needs to grow."

IF I COULD TURN

I've always wondered what I'd do if I

Was able to pause today and press rewind

To meet the younger you that I've only

seen through pictures when you reminisced on good times.

But I've made up my mind, on exactly how'd handle

Such a rare opportunity if it was granted.

First thing I'd do is take you by the hand and

lead you far away from the man that

Convinced you that your blessings were flaws

and rarities were faults

I'm thinking his vision was fogged

or he took his eye off the ball

The one he hit to get you,

but once he got you, he just walked.

All over your heart, because when you love

you love hard, he could tell from the start.

So he took advantage of that.

You were naïve so you believed

he wouldn't do you so bad.

He put his hands on you after promising

he would never do that but

you saw the good in people so you still took him back.

This time he kept his hands to himself and let his words
do the swinging.

Every syllable tightened around your throat till you
barely were breathing.

Sentences left your eyes swollen shut till you could no
longer see his

Tongue's next uppercut that would stop you from
dreaming

Treated your goals like a joke, and your hopes like a
punch line.

Your Momma noticed the difference but you told her you
were fine,

A line you'd perfected to make it through your days
without crying.

Self-esteem so low it hurt to look your reflection in the
eye,

But in due time, you got tired of trying. By then the
damage was done

Pieces of your heart shattered like broken glass, still
bleeding from the open cuts

It was either stitches of years of healing or quick fix to
close it up,

Which was cold, numb, don't give a fuck, middle finger
to love

You wanted whatever would keep you

from returning to that position

Of playing the fool again.

So you chose a life with no feelings.

So if I could turn back the hands of time,

I'd go back to when you made that decision

Wipe every tear from your face, hold you close,

and beg you to reconsider.

"If they weren't worth staying in your life, then they're not worth
preventing the right one from coming into your life."

DON'T GIVE UP

You never needed a guy with a lot of money.

He doesn't have to be a professional athlete

or drive some fancy car

Or take you expensive places.

You never lowered your standards.

You just realized

Those things aren't more important

Than someone who's ready to love you.

Ready to listen to you even when it's not convenient

And plan quality time with you without you having to
ask.

Somebody who finally has nothing to hide

Especially his feelings for you.

Because he shows them every chance he gets.

That's what really matters.

I mean, you've been dating the good-looking

"emotionally unavailable" men for too long.

Now it's time to find someone with room in their heart
for one,

and only one more.

Someone who's been waiting for you,

The way you're now waiting for him.

Give yourself another chance.

Don't give up.

When I speak messages to my future wife, a lot of people think I'm crazy for it, but I was always taught there was power in the tongue. If there's any kind of connection already between us, hopefully she can take comfort in the intentions of my heart that I'll only solidify with my actions once the time comes. But I believe in a woman whom God has set aside for me, and call me anxious, but I literally can't wait to speak to her. So I don't…

*"What's the point of being like everyone else
if nobody else is happy?"*

RELATIONSHIP GOALS

If we date, we're not dating to pass time
We're not dating just to be
a good look on our Timeline.
We're not dating just to be each other's
iPhone screensavers
Or to make our exes jealous by
showing them we've finally upgraded.

If we date, it's because
we're becoming best friends
Because our crowns coordinate
and we're both planning to win
If we date, it's bigger than just love alone

I want a family and spiritual partner.
If we date, we're dating to grow.

"I've lied to myself before, but my heart hasn't."

FAIR WARNING

I'm not the one you come to when you feel like
you're supposed to be perfect.
When you can't be scared of anything
Or not know what the future holds for certain.
I'm not the one you call when you
Need to be judged.
When you need someone to remind you
Of all the ways you keep messing up.
I'm not the one you talk to
When you hope to hear, "I told you so".
When you can't make mistakes
And aren't allowed the need to grow.

I'm the one you contact
When everything is all bad.

And part of it is your fault
But you still just need someone to have your back.
I'm the one you dial
When you don't want to be analyzed,
When you need freedom to just vent
Whether it be to scream, yell, or even cry.

I'm the place in your life
Where being real is the only rule.
Where how you feel is the only truth
Because I see the best in you.

"Some people plan ahead on how they're going to buy things to love.

I plan ahead on how I'm going to keep the one I love."

I PROMISE YOU TO NEVER

Let my masculinity dim the light of your femininity

Let my leadership negate the necessity of your wisdom

Let my protection infringe on your independence

Let my intentions stray from my actions

Let my ambition make me forget that you also deserve support

Let my strength mishandle your delicacy

Let my love be words alone

Or keep you from leaving me if I break any part of this promise.

"The lessons I learned were the lips I used to kiss her insecurities."

I GOT IT

Dear Future Wife,

You got insecurities?

I got kisses for that.

You got trust issues?

I got communication and consistency for that.

You got haters?

Then I got distance for that.

I'm not talking about running,

I'm talking about vacations to other islands

to make them even more mad.

You got a broken heart?

I got love and attention for that.

I got plans to spend my whole life with you
So we'll have time to put all those pieces right back.

"Without creativity and effort, you'll never experience love to its fullest potential."

TONIGHT

I don't wanna leave the house tonight

I just don't feel like going out tonight

Fuck the streets,

I'm tryna lay up with you tonight

I got a few ideas of better things to do tonight

Like turn up in another way,

pointing figures to pick a place to taste

Pull out the wine bottles

save the liquor for another day

I don't feel like

being in a crowded place

If we're going to be sweaty

I'd rather it be from lovemaking by the fireplace

I like the sound of my hips

dropping between your legs

Better than the DJ screaming

at us to wave our hands in the air.

I'd rather see your ankles spreading

By my ears instead.

I mean it might as well be worth it

if you plan on messing up your hair

But don't get me wrong,

it doesn't have to end with lovemaking

We can spend the evening

perfecting our love language

Sit in silence or talk for hours

about how the world was created

Because it's that real,

be it physical or mental stimulation

Let them keep the long lines

and "Free before 11's"

If they talk, let 'em talk.

We can be lame together.

"There's nothing like meeting someone who mentally gives you company

in places you've always felt alone."

SHE'S REAL

Some girls need a baller

because they're so high-maintenance.

She doesn't need a man for anything,

but still shows appreciation.

Some girls don't get treated right,

and get revenge by cheating.

If she ain't getting treated right,

she'll let you know by leaving.

Some girls will roll your weed for you,

and play video games.

She's going to make sure you eating right

and proofread your resumé.

For likes and comments,

some girls will take pictures of their ass.

She'd rather get looked over

and pose in pictures with class.

Some girls beg for attention by twerking,

and can bust it open.

She gets respect by working,

and would rather stay focused.

Some girls won't leave the house

unless their weave's tight in the lacefront.

She has so much confidence,

she comfortable with or without makeup.

Some girls dodge boredom

by giving any guy sex.

She'd rather be lonely

than settle for less.

Some girls strive to be

the baddest bitch they can be.

You call her bad or a bitch,

and watch how fast she'll leave.

Some girls beg for a ring

so they can get you for half.

She waits patiently then helps you

double what you already had.

Some girls make it clap, but she deserves an applause

'cause while she never could fit in,

she remained real through it all.

"All I need to have in common with you to love you is our definition of respect, love, and loyalty."

KNOW BETTER

You got a past?

I got a past too.

I put my trust in some

who put me through shit I thought

I wouldn't last through.

You made mistakes?

Well, I've probably made a few more.

Left some hearts scarred

Just from being emotionally immature.

You have regrets?
With me, they don't have to hide.
Let's both give ourselves a second chance
To know better this time.

"Tomorrow isn't promised, so good sex should be guaranteed."

TIME AND A PLACE

Yes, there's a time and a place to be chivalrous,
To have a nice dinner and light some candles.
Then there are times when your scent
gives me hunger pangs
Till I binge between your legs
like I've lost my manners
Where phone calls can wait,
A few lamps may break.
Don't trip, we'll have insurance.
Me, you, and my Timberland boots
Just for grip so you don't have to worry.
Water breaks while I'm slow-paced,
Tasting you will be my intermission.
Twelve rounds, I can go the distance
Till we both win by split decision.

You can cheer me on by screaming my name
Or stay silent and catch your breath
As you watch me work
Streetlights shining on me and you drenched in sweat.
See, there's a time and a place for making love
But never a time to leave with regrets
So I want to make the most of every moment
Because life's too short for boring sex.

"Only love me if I don't have to compete with their perception.

That's a battle I can't win and choose not to fight."

IF SHE'S PERFECT

If she's perfect, I'm not interested.

If she never wants to be left alone

Even without a valid reason.

If she never hopes I cancel my plans

To be with her because she's clingy.

If she never has a bad hair day

Despite having plenty of time to style it

If she never overreacts

And hopes I understand without her apologizing.

If she has no love handles, scars,

Nor could lose or gain a few pounds

And every pair of jeans she ever tries on

Fits just right, making her butt look perfectly round

And if she has absolutely no trust issues

From times she gave her all in the past

Then I don't want her.

I want someone to work, learn, and grow with,

Miss Perfect has no room to do any of that.

"Heaven isn't worth having unless

you can keep it forever. There's no way to prepare yourself

for the pain it takes to lose it. Love is no different."

I GOT A CONFESSION

Massages are my thing.
Well, giving them to be specific.
So if I don't let you sleep some nights without
Rubbing your feet, please don't be offended.
It's just my way of being selfish
In time, I hope you learn to accept it.
Oh, and those attitudes you like to catch,
Won't be enough to run me away.
In fact, I'll probably come after you
And kiss you until you agree to stay.
If it's really serious, then I'll clear my schedule,
sit quietly, and listen to you.

But if you were just in a bad mood,

Then we're having makeup sex and calling a truce.

I almost forgot, sometimes

I can be a bit protective.

Even when it comes to family and friends,

I won't let them disrespect you.

At times, I'll even get offended for you,

just remind me to stay cool

Unless we got bail money and

you don't mind me acting a fool.

One last thing, I really don't like to let go.

My heart doesn't start to stop,

it starts because it's made itself at home.

I believe in working things out,

Even when it gets hard,

So when our Honeymoon Phase is over,

Don't mind me if I keep finding new ways to press Restart.

The craziest thing about growth is seeing someone who reminds you of a younger you and being reminded of how far you've come. Not in a sense of looking down on them, but just gaining a new appreciation for your own journey while empathizing with their potential benefit from your direction but waiting until your help was solicited. To my surprise, a lot of guys were more open to hearing me speak on things going on in their personal lives, unlike the prideful position I maintained that I had the world figured out in fifteen short years. I could only remove so much bias as I remembered frankly the feelings of my own trial and error, and with that, I told them everything I had to learn the hard way with hopes of keeping them from feeling what I felt to find out.

"Trust his words over his actions if he says he doesn't want a relationship, but then acts like he does. Trust me, he meant his words."

SHE'S NOT THE ONE

She's not the one you date when

You're just looking to have fun.

She's not the one you want just for a night

Or the one you go to during your relationship "break".

She's not the one you want just to impress your boys

Or to make your ex jealous.

She's not the one you want when you just

Wanna "see what happens"

She's not the warm-up or the prep,

She's the one you prepare for,

The one you pray and wait for

And won't waste the opportunity with once

She gives it to you.

Because you know there won't ever be another her.

She's that one.

"The most loyal women ask for the simplest things.
They only seem complex to undeserving men."

IT'S NOT COMPLICATED

You'll buy her a gift

but won't pay her any attention

Said you would give her the world

but won't take time to listen

Now you got her feeling like

there's something she must be missing

When really you're just blinded to your diamond

all from those cubic zirconia's glisten.

Basically you make things more complicated

than it has to be

I'm no mathematician but this seems

like simple math to me.

Divide her burdens, multiply her joys,

But first inside the parentheses

You must subtract random girls, and your boys

who try to get you to do single things.

Once you've handled that

then come back to the addition

Of your time and loyalty,

match her effort and her ambition.

What that equals is two people

destined to go the distance

As for geometry just keep your circle as small

as the one at the end of the sentence.

Or else lame ass dudes will call you a square

because at the root of your actions

is a desire to reciprocate her heart in full

instead of in fractions

and fractured like, communication

when pride is involved

No Pythagorean Theorem but the right angle is

two who can admit they were wrong.

Nobody means to drive

on the median of any road

But when you wreck, the mode of transportation

still has to be towed.

Let me simplify that just in case

you missed the message:

Intentions don't mean a damn thing

after you've done the damage.

So if you really love this girl, cool,

make sure you show and prove.

Because if she's above average

best believe another man has noticed it too.

*"You can never give something that's good enough
to a guy who doesn't even know what he wants."*

WHY WOMEN DON'T GIVE MORE MEN A CHANCE

The average woman knows

there are some really good brothers

But for every one she's met,

There are ten more who'll ask for her number.

If she doesn't feel like talking,

they'll call her stuck-up and ugly

Then start fronting and saying

That they really didn't want her.

And probably nine more who'll try

and earn her trust just to lose it.

Because "he wasn't ready for a relationship",

and decided that after he screwed her.

Another eight who'll say they're single

and left their girl alone

When they're only on bad terms,

he just felt like being a hoe.

Seven more who'll send dick pics to chicks

who don't know 'em

But let her send one emoji,

then it'll be "these hoes ain't loyal"

They'll cheat 100 times

and still want forgiveness

But if she cheated once

they'll act like the world just ended.

Another six abusive types
Who're quick to smack a girl
But if a dude the same size tried 'em,
they wouldn't speak out of turn.

Five more who'll front on Instagram
like they're running things
Meanwhile, they still gotta ask their moms
if they can have company.
You know the kind that got a curfew,
but somehow "grind all day"?
And pretend they balling when really
they just ain't got bills to pay.

There'll be another four who'll claim they need a girl

with all her curves and edges

But can offer her nothing more

than community dick and bad credit.

At least three who'll have a sidechick

and have the nerve to be jealous

With reverse psychology pressing her

about who **she's** been texting.

That leaves two, who don't keep their word

but swear they keep it real

But nothing's real about a dude

who plays a girl that's loyal to him.

So for all those types, there's just one

who won't need third and fourth chances

The kind of man who doesn't come IN

emotionally damaged.

Who can earn her respect without having to demand it

Not only has big dreams

but also has a plan and

Can time manage so he doesn't get so busy,

she starts feeling stranded

But instead spoils her

with consistency and understanding.

And most importantly has morals

and still believes in marriage.

No, that doesn't mean he's perfect,

but he's still better than average,

And if she's bringing steak to the table,

Yes, she deserves a man bringing more than salad

Even if it means curving

most of them who come her way

Because it's easier to stay single

when you know the games people play.

"I would never try and dominate my wife.
That's not a relationship.

That's ownership. Make me better like I make you
better so we both win."

SUBMISSION

People interpret the Bible differently,

so referencing that won't help,

But submission is defined as obedience

and accepting the control of someone else.

So if a woman submits to her husband,

then it is what is.

That means she shuts the hell up

and puts her judgment second to his.

The problem is

even good men get off track sometimes,

So why would her only mental contribution

be a cosign?

I've always thought the best relationships

happened when neither side

Needed to dominate the other

in order for them to thrive.

I would much rather my role

as a man be synonymous

With elevation, edification, encouragement,

and empowerment

Control and dominance

may work well for coward men

But for those of us trying to win,

it don't make a lot of sense.

'Cause some things we're not equipped with,

like a woman's intuition

Their perspectives, wisdom,

and their unique experiences.

So I'd never choose a woman

who just stays out of the way

Over a woman who can respectfully

check me when I'm trippin'.

I won't feel emasculated

by my regard for her opinion

And my ego's not so fragile

that I have to limit her potential.

It's not a threat to my manliness

to ask that her submission

Not be to my gender,

but to both of our best interests.

I can still provide, protect,

and defend her honor

Without treating her discernment for us

as a mere option

Or secondary to mine,

playing backup, or just the alternate.

No one on our team should be second string,

we'll win or lose as starters.

So if a man earns a woman's respect,

he won't need her submission

Long as he's on the right path

then she's going to ride with 'em.

The idea comes from a time

when women only cooked and cleaned

But evolved men need a life partner,

not life employees.

"I guess it's easier to say, 'I get hoes' than to admit you had a good girl but you couldn't keep her happy."

IT AIN'T WORTH IT

Better than good enough was the agreement,

perfection was the goal

Because you felt like with all that she came with,

she deserved all you had and more

So putting a smile on her face was cool,

but if you could go over and beyond

You'd reach for the stars and shine light

on the darkest corners of her soul.

Somewhere along the way things changed and

you couldn't retrace your steps

DERRICK JAXN

To see where you dropped the ball

on things you once felt

She seemed a little less exciting

and more irritated with you.

At times it got so bad you couldn't even stand

to be in the same room.

But what you don't understand

is this is how love goes

That relationships come with thorns

just as well as the rose,

But you're so ready to act on your misperception

of something real

Going back out to chase the fantasy

you expected to live.

Ready to put it all on the line,

ready to risk it all,

Ready to let temptation exploit your weakness

because your word isn't strong,

Ready to let her learn to live without you

until she's in another man's arms.

Just remember, only a fool wins the lotto

and continues to play with scratch-offs.

"She's not trying to blame you for mistakes her ex made, but she's not trying to go through the same shit over and over again either."

TWELVE THINGS SHE WISHES YOU UNDERSTOOD

She's a lover but she'll fight for you.

Even when she feels like she can't no more,

she'll still try for you.

She's not jealous,

but she didn't fall in love with plans of letting go

So when other girls cross the line,

she expects YOU to let 'em know.

She's not stupid,

she was allowing you to earn her trust

With hopes you'd appreciate it too much

to do things to mess it up.

She's not needy,

but she deserves to be a priority of your attention

Especially when she ignores it from other guys

who can't wait to catch you slippin'.

She's not insecure,

but she wants to know that you find her attractive.

The way you look at and touch her

should all scream how glad you are to have her.

She's not rushing things,

she just doesn't have time to be playing games.

She's trying to build an empire with somebody

who's trying to do the same.

She's not judging you,

she just realizes your potential

And won't waste time if you're not trying

because she only dates men with ambition.

She doesn't have trust issues,

but won't put up with all the lies.

If honesty is too much to ask

then you shouldn't have even bothered to say hi.

She loves the thought of being yours only,

but not when you're for everybody else

Not when new numbers are popping up in your phone,

not when you're deleting texts.

She's not too sensitive, she has feelings she shows to you

'cause you're her man,

And it doesn't mean she's not making sense

just because you don't understand.

She knows she complicated,

so if you're not ready, just say it

So she can save you both the trouble

of you coming around when she's done waiting.

"The best way to get what you want is not to ask, but rather to put the things you don't want on the list of things you will not tolerate.."

DECLINED

Having sufficient funds is
required for any transaction.
You can't buy anything if
you have a zero balance.
Before you go to make the purchase
You must make the required deposit
Because nothing's more embarrassing
Than the sound of your card declining.

Same thing when it comes to
courting a real woman.
Except her value won't be based
On things that are materialistic.

If you can't tell the truth
Then the sale won't go through.
If you play games and neglect her
Then your PIN won't be accepted.
If you don't have a relationship with God
Expect to have your card declined,
But don't expect more than one swipe
Because you'll only hold up the line.

*"The real drawback to cheating is that oftentimes
you end up getting a good girl to cheat on.
And once you burn that bridge, it's gone."*

SHOULD'VE, COULD'VE,
WOULD'VE

Should've let her have the last word

Instead of tryna have the last laugh.

Maybe you would've bit your tongue

If you realized some words

you just can't take back.

Should've valued the fact that she believed in you

And would listen to you go on and on

about your dreams.

Should've seen that you had a real one

The way that she was committed to you
even without a ring.

Should've accepted the harsh truths
Even when you didn't want to hear them
Should've known she wouldn't tell you
anything to hurt you
Only things to help you
realize your potential.

You could've been relaxing right now
Feeding strawberries to her
in a bath of bubbles,
Enjoying the fruits of your success
With the woman who stuck by you
when you had nothing.

You could've been picking out baby names
And making plans for a home with more room.

You could've been waking up at night
Kissing her stomach every time the baby moved.

You could've let your boys leave without you.
Yeah, they would've called you lame for it,
But you just couldn't say no
Once they told you there'd be girls over.

Could've walked away
And went back home to what was already yours
If you would've known that ignorance isn't bliss
It's the quiet before the storm

Should've listened to your mom's warnings
Should've known that you wouldn't be different
Should've known that once your actions spoke hatred
No amount of "I'm sorrys" would make her listen.

Should've known that tears don't last forever
And when they stop, so do second chances.
Should've known that once a good girl walks out
She's won't be taking any steps backwards.

Should've known, could've done better
And right now your worst nightmare
wouldn't be coming true
You reading this poem thinking about her and
Her new man, wishing it was you.

There's not enough time in a day nor words in the dictionary to fully explain who I am. But through my story, I can only hope you've gotten enough to help you as you continue writing your own. At times, what people see makes them curious why I think I'm so perfect at "love" and the obvious answer is that I'm not perfect at it. I just believe in it. And while I may not know everything, there are some things in which I have no doubt.

"Know when people are down for you, and when people are down for what you can do for them."

WHATEVER IT COSTS

They're going to call you stuck-up.
They're going to ask why you don't give them a chance.
They're going to ask you who you think you are
After assuming that you think you're all that.
When they realize your standards,
They're going to be intimidated.
They're going to wonder what happened
When their inconsistency isn't tolerated.
They're going to walk away from you
And it's going to be their loss
Because real men will see your worth
And pay whatever it costs.

"Your 'type' could be what's keeping you from your soulmate."

HE SHOULD

He may not be the most talented
Or stand six feet tall.
He may not wear expensive cologne
Or drive the latest car.
But he should be too protective
To let any man disrespect you.
And too busy with loving you
To let anything else make him neglect you.
He should stay when you need somebody
To just hold you for a while.
He should try to make corny jokes
When it's been too long since you've smiled.
He should know, that even if he does make it

And gets rich and successful.
That none of it will matter to you
More than consistency and effort.

"In life, you have to nurture what you want.
You can't water the weeds and wonder what happened to the
roses."

THANK YOU

I was sitting in a café'
the other day
Halfway minding my business
as I heard a woman say
"These days, men don't know a
good thing till it's gone
Hoes is winning while all us
good women are alone."
And it seems she's got a point,
I gotta admit
We're quick to diss a girl with standards
for one who's licking her lips.
We'll look over Mrs. Right

for Mrs. Right now
But get our feelings hurt when our daughter
grows up and gets turned out
So let me say this, to all the good women;
Thank you
Thank you for the pain you felt
that you refused to let change you.
Thank you for having a body
that could stop traffic
But making a man prove he was worthy
before he could romance it.
Thank you for looking up to the
Lauryn Hills and Lisa Bonets
The Erykah Badus, Jill Scotts,
and Janelle Monaes
Thank you for all the trends that came along
that you didn't follow
And for cutting off guys who tried to buy you.
Thank you for making it just fine without 'em.
Thank you for the friends you cut off
who were content being average.
Thank you for the guys you didn't entertain

who had no interest in marriage.
Thank you for the late-night hours you spent at work
while everyone else was getting turnt.
Thank you for waking up in the morning
and still going to church.
Thank you for the all-nighters you pulled
when it was time to take the finals.
Thank you for the resumes and applications
you submitted to get a job after college.
Thank you for leveraging your mind
when so many sell their body.
Thank you for loving yourself
as a middle finger to society.
Just to be clear, this isn't a knock on sisters
who took a different route.
This is just proof there are men
who love what you're about.

"Be willing to sacrifice anyone who's causing you to sacrifice yourself to love them."

KEEP ON

Keep ignoring the red flags.
He'll keep flying them high.
Give him your trust more than twice.
He'll make you build it a third time.
His side pieces will stick around
if you're proud to be the "main chick".
If you're satisfied with him just coming home to you,
He'll keep you from men to build a home with.
Keep making false threats,
He'll keep telling false truths.
Keep accepting the games he plays,
He'll keep handing the controller to you.

"Nothing like a woman who loves herself too much to remain in the company

of those who don't appreciate her."

FIRST THINGS FIRST

If he's moving too slow on locking you down,

Then pump his brakes on seeing you naked.

If he thinks you're trying to rush him into a commitment

Then let him make love to his patience.

If he's doesn't want to turn a house into a home

Then he doesn't need to spend the night.

Don't let him lay a finger on you

If he hasn't first caressed your mind.

If he's too young to have a title

because he's still enjoying his "prime"

Then move on, because you're too grown

To let anyone waste your time.

"I'll burn a bridge before I get walked all over."

MOVING ON

Busted windows won't be necessary.
Neither will sleeping with one of his friends.
Moving on, doing better, and forgetting
Him is the best revenge.
Ignore calls from his mom,
She's a woman, she'll understand.
Nothing personal, but when you cut someone off
Sometimes you can't leave a single strand.
Delete his number, texts, and pictures,
And anything else you got of his since you met him.
No need to clutter your heart with belongings
from a guest who overstayed his welcome.
Get back to loving you with quality time

And refocusing on being your own upgrade
Because moving on isn't easy
But you're worth whatever time it takes.

"Time heals everything except immaturity.
Only growth can fix that."

TOO OLD

There comes a time when we're too old for
"We'll cross that bridge when we get there."
"Let's just see what happens."
"A bond is stronger than a title."
"I'm not really trying to get married."
"Can you come over and kick it?"
"When me and you gon' finally chill?"
"I forgot my wallet, you got me?
I'll pay you back, you know how it is."
"I'll go look for a job tomorrow."
"Nobody out here hiring."
"I don't need a plan for my future,
One more mixtape and I'm bound to get signed."

Dear Queen, time is precious, so is your love
Neither one of those should be wasted.
A man is either planning to protect your crown
Or planning to break it.

"You can't keep what you didn't prepare for, and you can't prepare for what you lost faith would come."

YOU STILL DESERVE IT

You didn't cry yourself to sleep
all those nights for nothing
Or suffer consequences of
choosing your ex to trust in
Or ignore passes from guys who
wanted what was between your legs
Or press delete on all the
disingenuous "Hey stranger" texts
Or curl up on Friday nights,
just you and your remote
Because boys in your generation
forgot what it meant to court
Or fall back from the guy
who really had potential

Because he was attractive,
but couldn't keep up with your mental
Or go on dead-end dates,
receiving backhanded compliments
Or offer to pay for yourself when
you realized he was expecting sex
Or survive the embarrassment
of your business being told
By a guy you gave some to who was so proud
he let all his friends know
Or move on from those who wanted
to jeopardize your future
By having no plan for their own
except one to use you
Or cut off all the ones who wanted
you to chase them
Or almost give it up too soon,
but still resist the temptation
Or get your hopes up just to
eventually see their true colors
Or find peace with not settling
if it meant getting looked over.

No, you went through all of that because
deep down you knew you were worth it
And everything you've nearly given up on,
just know you still deserve it.

ACKNOWLEDGEMENTS

I did it. I finally did it. I completed college and had a job offer waiting for me as a territory sales manager for a major tobacco company. Sure, it was a controversial industry but the company had better pay and benefits than any job my friends or family members had. Free car. Free and unlimited gas card. Health and Dental. 401k and more.

In this economy, this was a sweet deal and I would be set for life once I retired. All I had to do was go to work, follow the script, and be a regular person. Except there was an irregular passion in me that wouldn't let me sleep some nights or hold my tongue most days. Social media was the closest thing I had to scratching the itch but even that didn't quite do it. Then finally, I realized it was my purpose as an author that was waiting for me to find and nurture it with everything I had.

So I did...sorta. I also held on to my job. After all, I went through 18 years of schooling, a challenging internship, and a 4-level interview process to get it. But there was someone who showed me that there would only be room for one. A brand new manager looking for any and everything to change with my unit to help solidify her importance with the company.

She must've seen the desire to write books in my half-assing on the job or short attention span during unit meetings because she began making life miserable with every condescending email and micro managing phone call to keep tabs on me until I finally got to the point where even I had to admit I could not do both job and passion. I'd have to choose one.

So here I am. Devoid of the job I thought would take me into my retirement and now living a life I only salivated for just a year ago. So, I'd like to take this opportunity to acknowledge my former manager. You were quite the blessing in disguise.

CPSIA information can be obtained at www.ICGtesting.com
Printed in the USA
LVOW11s1143120815

449654LV00004B/6/P

9 780991 033638